THE INDIAN SPORTS

AN INSIGHT INTO THE HISTORY AND SIGNIFICANCE OF INDIAN TRADITIONAL SPORTS

DR. JAGADEESH PILLAI

|| Dedicated to all wisdom seekers around the World ||

৸৹

Contents

Contents

Prayer

"Om Bhadram Karnebhih Shrunuyaama DevaahBhadram Pashyemaakshabhiryajatraah SthirairangaistushtuvaamsastanoobhihVyashema Devahitam YadaayuhSwasti Na Indro VridhashravaahSwasti Nah Pooshaa VishwavedaahSwasti Nastaarkshyo ArishtanemihSwasti No Brihaspatir DadhaatuOm Shantih, Shantih, Shantih"

The literal meaning of this mantra is: OM. O Gods! Let us hear auspicious words from our ears. O reverent Gods! Let us behold propitious visions from our eyes, let our organs and body be stable, healthy, and strong. Let us do that which is pleasing to the gods in the life span allotted to us. May Indra, inscribed in the scriptures, bring us fortune! May Pushan, the knower of the world, grant us prosperity! May Trakshya, who vanquishes enemies, bestow us with blessings! May Brihaspati bring us success!
OM Peace, Peace, Peace.

About the Author

Dr. Jagadeesh Pillai is a renowned Guinness World Record holder, writer, and researcher hailing from Varanasi, also known as the abode of Lord Shiva. With a Ph.D. in Vedic Science and a range of creative ideas and achievements, he is a true polymath. He is the author of more than 100 books including Research Publications. Although his roots can be traced back to Kerala, the people of Varanasi hold him in high regard and affectionately consider him one of their own.

In 1998, Dr. Pillai was offered a job at Banaras Hindu University, but he left the position after only two months to pursue greater goals in life. He believed that in order to study Indian scriptures and engage in other creative endeavours, he needed to retire from the daily grind of working solely for money at a young age.

He started an export business from scratch, using the knowledge he had gained from a previous job in the industry. His intelligence and unique approach to business led to great success in a short period of time, earning him more in just a decade and a half than he would have in a lifetime working in a government job. Upon the passing of Dr. APJ Abdul Kalam, Dr. Pillai decided to leave the business and dedicate himself to reading, studying, researching, and experimenting.

During his tenure in the export business, Dr. Pillai traveled to over 16 countries, gaining valuable insight and experiencing the world and life in detail.

Dr. Pillai has achieved four Guinness World Records in the following subjects:

"Script to Screen" - In this record, Dr. Pillai produced and directed an animation film within the shortest time possible, breaking the previous record set by Canadians. He has also received numerous national and international awards and recognitions for this achievement.

Longest Line of Postcards - For this record, Dr. Pillai created a line of 16,300 postcards on the occasion of the 163rd anniversary of Indian Postal Day. The event also included a questionnaire about the Indian flag.

Largest Poster Awareness Campaign - Dr. Pillai designed an awareness campaign on the subject of "Beti Bachao - Beti Padhao" (Save the Girl Child - Educate the Girl Child) to achieve this record.

Largest Envelope - In tribute to the Indian Prime Minister's "Make in India" initiative, Dr. Pillai created a 4000 square meter envelope using waste paper to achieve this record.

Attempted - **70000 Candles on a 210 kg Cake** - To celebrate the 70th Indian Independence Day, Dr. Pillai attempted to light 70,000 candles on a 210 kg cake, which was recorded in World Records India.

Attempted - **Documentary on Dhamek Stupa of Sarnath in 17 Languages** - Dr. Pillai attempted to create a documentary on the Dhamek Stupa of Sarnath, dubbing it in 17 different languages. The result of this attempt is currently awaiting confirmation from the Guinness World Records.

Dr. Pillai is skilled in teaching the Bhagavad Gita, a Hindu scripture, and is popular among young people. He has helped many young people improve their lives through his motivational teachings.

In addition to teaching, he has composed and sung numerous Sanskrit Bhajans and patriotic songs.

He has also written and directed several short films and documentaries for awareness campaigns, and has volunteered with the police in both UP and Kerala to spread awareness about various issues through videos and photography.

Incredibly, he has produced and directed over 100 documentaries about the city of Varanasi, all on his own.

He has also helped and guided more than 25 boys and girls to achieve world records through creative and innovative methods. He is a multifaceted person who uses his intellect and the blessings given to him by God to excel in various areas. He is both a teacher and a student, always learning and teaching, and is able to master any subject he comes across.

He is a selfless social activist and motivational speaker who has overcome struggles and failures to become a successful and enthusiastic individual with a rich life experience.

In addition to his work with the Bhagavad Gita, he is also an efficient Tarot card reader, Astro-Vastu consultant, and a talented singer and composer. He has sung the entire Ram Charita Manas and Bhagavad Gita in his own compositions, and has sung the phrase "Lokah Samastha Sukhino Bhavantu" in 50 different languages. He is currently working on a detailed and scientific study of Vedas, Upanishads, Puranas, and the Bhagavad Gita. He has also composed and sung the Hanuman Chalisa and Gayatri Mantra in 108 and 1008 different compositions, respectively.

Awards - Four Times Guinness World Records, Winner of Mahatma Gandhi Vishwa Shanti Puraskar, Mahatma Gandhi Global Peace Ambassador, Kashi Ratna Award, Dr. APJ Abdul Kalam Motivational Person of the Year 2017, Mother Teresa Award, Indira Gandhi Priyadarshini Award, Bharat Vikas Ratna Award, Udyog Ratna Award, Vigyan Prasar Award, Poorvanchal Ratn Samman.

PREFACE

Sports have always been an integral part of Indian culture. For centuries, Indians have enjoyed various traditional sports and games as a way to stay active, build relationships, and foster a sense of camaraderie. My goal for this book, The Indian Sports: An Insight into the History and Significance of Indian Traditional Sports, is to explore the history and significance of Indian traditional sports and the many ways in which they have shaped Indian culture and society.

This book is intended to serve as an introduction to the rich history and culture of Indian sports for readers who are new to the subject. It explores the evolution of Indian sports from its traditional roots to its modern-day forms. The book covers various topics, including the development of different sports and games, the influence of religion on Indian sports, and the impact of the Indian Olympic team. It also examines the economics of Indian sports and the legacy of Indian sports in modern-day India.

The book draws on research from a variety of sources, including interviews with key figures in the Indian sports industry, archival materials, and cultural analysis. I have also conducted extensive field research in India, including attending sports games, interviewing athletes, and visiting locations associated with the production of Indian sports. Through this research, I hope to provide readers with a comprehensive understanding of the Indian sports industry and its various components.

I am deeply passionate about the history and significance of Indian sports and hope that this book will help to spread the appreciation of this wonderful tradition. I believe that Indian sports have a great deal to offer to the world and I am excited to share its cultural and historical significance with my readers.

I
Introduction to Indian Sports

India has a rich and diverse sports culture that has been an integral part of its society for centuries. From ancient times, sports have been a means of physical and mental development, recreation, and competition. The traditional sports of India not only reflect the country's cultural and historical heritage but also its unique customs, values, and beliefs.

The history of Indian sports can be traced back to the Vedic era when physical activities were an essential part of Hindu religious rituals. The ancient Indian epic, the Mahabharata, mentions several games such as dice, chess, and martial arts, which were popular among the people. The Mughal era saw the introduction of new sports such as polo, wrestling, and horse racing, which blended with the existing Indian sports to create a unique cultural identity.

The British Raj brought several Western sports to India, such as cricket, football, and hockey, which became popular among the Indian people and are now widely considered as national sports. However, the traditional Indian sports continued to thrive, especially in rural areas, and are still an essential part of the Indian culture.

Traditional Indian Sports

Kabaddi:

Kabaddi is a contact sport that originated in ancient India and is still widely played in rural areas. The game is played between two teams of seven players each, and the objective is for a player to raid the opponent's half and touch as many players as possible before returning to their half without getting caught. Kabaddi has gained popularity in recent years and is now played at the national and international level.

Pachisi:

Pachisi, also known as ludo, is a board game that is believed to have originated in ancient India. The game is played by four players with pieces that are moved according to the roll of dice. Pachisi is still played in rural areas and is a popular pastime among families and friends.

Gilli Danda:

Gilli Danda is a popular traditional sport that is played with two sticks, a small one called gilli and a larger one called danda. The objective of the game is to hit the gilli as far as possible with the danda and then run between two markers before the gilli is retrieved. Gilli Danda is widely played in rural areas and is a simple and fun sport that requires minimal equipment.

Mallakhamb:

Mallakhamb is a traditional Indian sport that combines gymnastics and wrestling. The sport is performed on a vertical pole or a rope and involves a series of acrobatic moves and holds. Mallakhamb is a physically demanding sport that requires strength, flexibility, and balance, and is considered a test of a person's athletic abilities.

Rural Olympics:

The Rural Olympics, also known as the Kila Raipur Sports Festival, is an annual event that showcases the traditional sports of rural India. The festival is held in the village of Kila Raipur in Punjab and attracts participants from all over India. The Rural Olympics include events such as tractor racing, bullock cart racing, and mallakhamb, and are a celebration of the rich sports culture of rural India.

Significance of Indian Traditional Sports

Indian traditional sports are more than just physical activities; they are a reflection of the country's cultural and historical heritage. These sports are an integral part of the Indian identity and are a source of pride and national unity. They also promote physical and mental well-being and foster a sense of community and teamwork.

In rural areas, traditional sports play a crucial role in the lives of people and are a means of recreation and entertainment. They are often played during festivals and other celebrations and bring people together to participate in friendly competition. These sports are also an important part of the rural economy, as they attract tourists and provide livelihood opportunities for those involved in their organization and promotion.

In addition to their cultural and social significance, traditional Indian sports also have a significant impact on the economy. The growth of traditional sports has created new employment opportunities, particularly in rural areas, and has contributed to the development of sports tourism. The promotion of traditional sports also helps to preserve the country's cultural heritage and provides a platform for young people to showcase their athletic abilities.

Indian traditional sports are an integral part of the country's cultural and historical heritage and play a significant role in the lives of its people. These sports reflect the country's unique customs, values, and beliefs and promote physical and mental well-being. They also contribute to the economy and help to preserve the country's cultural heritage. The promotion of traditional sports is an important aspect of the development of sports in India and provides a platform for young people to showcase their athletic abilities. The "The Indian Sports: An Insight into the History and Significance of Indian Traditional Sports" aims to provide a comprehensive understanding of the rich and diverse sports culture of India and its significance in shaping the country's identity.

"Sports is a reflection of the soul of a nation, and in India, sports have a soul as rich and diverse as the country itself."

৺

II

History of Indian Sports

The history of sports in India dates back thousands of years, with evidence of physical activities and games being played in ancient times. From religious rituals to competitive events, sports have been an integral part of Indian society for centuries. In this chapter, we will delve into the rich history of Indian sports, tracing its evolution from ancient times to the present day.

Ancient India

The earliest evidence of sports in India can be traced back to the Vedic era, around 1500 BCE. Physical activities and games were an essential part of Hindu religious rituals, with references to these activities being made in the Vedas and other Hindu scriptures. The Mahabharata, an ancient Indian epic, mentions several games such as dice, chess, and martial arts, which were popular among the people.

Physical fitness was highly valued in ancient India, and physical activities were an important part of education. Wrestling, archery, and chariot racing were among the most popular sports of the time, and were often used as training exercises for soldiers. The ancient Indian epic, the Ramayana, mentions the game of gatka, which is a form of martial arts still practiced in India today.

Medieval India

The Mughal era, which lasted from the 16th to the 19th century, saw the introduction of new sports such as polo, wrestling, and horse racing. These sports blended with the existing Indian sports to create a unique cultural identity. During this time, sports were an important part of the Mughal court, with the rulers and nobles participating in and sponsoring various sporting events.

The Mughal emperors also encouraged the development of sports facilities, such as stadiums and gymnasiums, which allowed people to participate in physical activities and games. This era also saw the introduction of new sports equipment, such as leather balls and metal clubs, which improved the quality of the games and made them more competitive.

British Raj

The British Raj, which lasted from the 18th to the mid-20th century, brought several Western sports to India, such as cricket, football, and hockey. These sports quickly gained popularity among the Indian people and are now widely considered as national sports. The British also introduced organized sports events, such as the All India Football Tournament and the Hockey tournament, which helped to promote the growth of these sports.

However, the traditional Indian sports continued to thrive during this time, especially in rural areas. The British Raj also saw the development of new sports facilities and the formation of sports clubs and organizations, which helped to promote the growth of sports in India.

Post-Independence

After India gained independence in 1947, the country made significant progress in the development of sports. The government established a sports department and introduced policies and programs to promote the growth of sports in the country. The creation of the National Sports Federations, which were responsible for the development of specific sports, helped to improve the quality of sports in India.

The 1980s and 1990s saw a significant increase in the popularity of sports in India, with the introduction of new sporting events and the establishment of new sports facilities. The growth of television and the media also helped to promote sports in India, and the country has produced several world-class athletes who have represented India on the international stage.

The history of sports in India is rich and diverse, reflecting the country's cultural and historical heritage. From ancient times to the present day, sports have been an integral part of

Indian society, promoting physical and mental well-being and fostering a sense of community and teamwork. The growth of sports in India has also had a significant impact on the economy, creating employment opportunities and contributing to the development of sports tourism.

The evolution of Indian sports is a testament to the country's rich cultural heritage and its ability to adapt and incorporate new elements while preserving its traditional sports. The introduction of Western sports and the growth of modern facilities and infrastructure have helped to bring Indian sports to the international stage, showcasing the country's athletic talent and its commitment to promoting sports.

The history of Indian sports also highlights the important role that sports play in promoting national unity and fostering a sense of pride in the country. From ancient religious rituals to modern-day international competitions, sports have brought people together, creating a sense of community and fostering a sense of belonging.

The history of Indian sports is an important aspect of the country's cultural and historical heritage and provides valuable insights into the evolution of sports in India. The "The Indian Sports: An Insight into the History and Significance of Indian Traditional Sports" aims to provide a comprehensive understanding of the rich and diverse history of Indian sports and its significance in shaping the country's identity.

"The legacy of Indian sports is not just about victories and records, but about the values and traditions that have been passed down through generations."

III

Traditional Indian Sports and Games

India is a land of rich cultural heritage and diverse traditions, and this is reflected in the wide range of traditional sports and games that have been passed down from generation to generation. In this chapter, we will explore some of the most popular traditional Indian sports and games, highlighting their history, rules, and significance.

Kabaddi

Kabaddi is a sport that originated in ancient India and is widely played in rural areas. The game is played between two teams, with each team taking turns to send a player, known as a raider, into the opponent's half to score points. The objective of the game is to touch as many opponents as possible and return to one's own half without being tackled.

Kabaddi is a physically demanding sport that requires speed, agility, and endurance. It is also a sport that requires teamwork, as the raider must rely on their team to protect them from being tackled. The sport is widely popular in India and is played at both the amateur and professional level.

Khokho

Khokho is a traditional Indian sport that is played in rural areas and is popular in the states of Maharashtra, Madhya Pradesh, and Uttar Pradesh. The game is played between two teams, with each team taking turns to defend and attack. The objective of the game is to strike the opponent's sticks with a stick while protecting one's own sticks.

Khokho is a physically demanding sport that requires speed, agility, and strength. It is also a sport that requires strategy, as players must coordinate their movements and tactics to outmaneuver the opponent. The sport is a popular pastime in rural India and is played by people of all ages.

Pachisi

Pachisi is an ancient Indian board game that is played using a board and pawns. The game is played between two to four players, with each player taking turns to move their pawns along the board. The objective of the game is to be the first player to move all of their pawns to the finish.

Pachisi is a game of strategy and skill that requires players to think ahead and make strategic moves. The game is widely played in India and is a popular pastime for families and friends. The game is also a popular tourist attraction, with many hotels and resorts offering Pachisi boards for guests to play on.

Gilli Danda

Gilli Danda is a traditional Indian sport that is played using two sticks, a small stick known as a gilli and a larger stick known as a danda. The game is played between two players, with each player taking turns to hit the gilli with the danda and score runs. The objective of the game is to be the player with the highest score at the end of the game.

Gilli Danda is a sport that requires hand-eye coordination and agility. The sport is widely played in rural India and is a popular pastime for children and adults. The sport is also a symbol of rural India, representing the country's cultural heritage and traditions.

Traditional Indian sports and games are an important part of the country's cultural heritage and provide valuable insights into the country's history and traditions. These sports and games are played by people of all ages and are a testament to the country's love of physical activity and competition.

It is essential to recognize that while many of these classic sports and games have been passed down through the ages, they are also susceptible to transformation and development as time progresses. As our society and culture evolve, so too do the rules and regulations of these beloved activities, allowing them to remain relevant and enjoyable for generations to come.

"Wrestling, archery, horse riding, and
martial arts are just a few examples of the
traditional sports that have shaped the
cultural identity of India."

૪૭

IV

The Role of Religion in Indian Sports

Religion has played a significant role in the development and practice of traditional sports in India. From ancient times, sports were not just physical activities, but also had spiritual and cultural significance. Many traditional sports in India were associated with religious festivals and rituals, and were considered a way of offering tribute to the gods.

One of the most famous examples of the intersection of religion and sports in India is the game of Kabaddi. Originating in the Indian subcontinent, the game was played as a part of harvest festivals and was considered a way to seek the blessings of the gods for a good harvest. The game was also associated with Hindu mythology and was said to have been played by Lord Hanuman and his army of monkeys.

Another example is the game of Mallakhamb, a traditional Indian sport that involves performing acrobatic and gymnastic feats on a vertical pole or a rope. The sport is believed to have originated in the 12th century and was initially performed by Hindu ascetics as a form of physical and spiritual discipline. Even today, Mallakhamb is practiced as a spiritual and meditative discipline, with participants performing the sport as a form of offering to the gods.

Similarly, the sport of Silambam, which originated in South India, was also associated with Hindu mythology.

The sport involves the use of a bamboo stick as a weapon, and was considered a way to train soldiers in ancient times. It was also performed as a part of religious festivals and was believed to bring good luck and prosperity.

Religion has also played a role in shaping the rules and regulations of traditional sports in India. For example, in the game of Kabaddi, there are strict rules regarding the use of foul language and physical contact, which are meant to promote respect and fairness among players. These rules are rooted in the principles of Hinduism, which emphasizes non-violence and respect for others.

In addition to shaping the rules of traditional sports, religion has also influenced the attitudes of athletes and fans towards sports in India. Many athletes see their participation in sports as a way to honor their gods and to express their devotion. Fans, too, view sports as a way to connect with their religion and to find a deeper meaning in their lives.

Religion has played a crucial role in the development and practice of traditional sports in India. From shaping the rules and regulations of sports to influencing the attitudes of athletes and fans, religion has played a significant role in shaping the sports culture in India. Today, traditional sports continue to be an important part of Indian religious and cultural life, serving as a testament to the deep connection between sports and spirituality in India.

"The athleticism and skill displayed by Indian athletes in modern sports is a testament to the country's rich athletic heritage."

೪෬

V

Indian Sports and the Olympics

The Olympic Games, held every four years, are the world's largest and most prestigious international sports competition. They have been a platform for athletes from all over the world to showcase their skills and to compete at the highest level. India, with its rich history and diverse culture, has been an active participant in the Olympic Games since the early 1900s.

India made its Olympic debut in 1900, when Norman Pritchard, an Anglo-Indian athlete, participated in the Paris Olympics and won two silver medals in Athletics. Since then, India has participated in every Summer Olympics, except for two editions – the 1976 Montreal Games and the 1980 Moscow Games – where it boycotted the event due to political reasons.

Despite India's long history of participation in the Olympic

Games, the country's performance has been relatively modest compared to other countries. India has won a total of 28 Olympic medals, including 9 gold medals, and most of these medals have been won in field hockey. The Indian field hockey team dominated the sport in the early decades of the 20th century, winning six consecutive gold medals from 1928 to 1956.

In recent years, however, India's performance in the Olympics has improved, and the country has won medals in a variety of sports, including shooting, wrestling, boxing, and badminton. The rise of Indian sports can be attributed to the increasing investment in sports infrastructure and the growth of private sports academies.

One of the most notable Olympic achievements by an Indian athlete was Abhinav Bindra's gold medal in the 10m air rifle event at the 2008 Beijing Olympics. Bindra's win marked India's first individual gold medal in the Olympic Games and was a major milestone in the country's sports history.

Despite these achievements, India still faces challenges in its quest for Olympic glory. One of the biggest challenges is the lack of resources and infrastructure for sports development. Additionally, there is a lack of support for athletes, particularly in rural areas, and a lack of recognition for their achievements.

To address these challenges, the Indian government and sports organizations have started investing in sports infrastructure and promoting sports education. They have also started to provide support and recognition for athletes, which has led to an improvement in India's performance in international sports events, including the Olympics.

India has a long and proud history of participation in the Olympic Games. Despite modest success in the past, India's performance in the Olympics has improved in recent years due to increased investment in sports infrastructure and the growth of private sports academies. With the right support and resources, India has the potential to become a major player in the world of sports and to win more Olympic medals in the years to come.

"Sport is a mirror that reflects the soul of a nation, and the legacy of Indian sports is one of determination, strength, and resilience."

৪৩

VI
Popular Indian Sports and their Influencers

India is a diverse country with a rich sporting heritage, and the nation has produced many talented athletes and sports influencers over the years. From cricket to badminton and from football to wrestling, India has a thriving sports culture that is beloved by millions of fans across the country. In this chapter, we will explore some of the most popular Indian sports and the influencers who have made a significant impact in each of these sports.

Cricket:

Cricket is arguably the most popular sport in India, and the country has a long and proud history in the sport. The first recorded cricket match in India was played in 1721, and since then, the sport has grown in popularity and become a crucial part of Indian culture.

One of the biggest influencers in Indian cricket is Sachin Tendulkar. Nicknamed the 'God of Cricket', Tendulkar is widely regarded as one of the greatest batsmen of all time. He made his international debut for India at the age of 16 and went on to play for the country for over two decades, scoring over 100 international centuries and setting numerous records in the process.

Another influential figure in Indian cricket is Kapil Dev. Dev was the captain of the Indian cricket team that won the 1983 Cricket World Cup, a historic moment that is still remembered and celebrated in India today. He is widely regarded as one of the best all-rounders to have played the sport and was inducted into the International Cricket Council's Hall of Fame in 2010.

Badminton:

Badminton is another sport that has a long history in India and is widely played and watched across the country. The sport has produced many talented athletes over the years, and several Indian players have become international stars in the sport.

One of the biggest influencers in Indian badminton is Prakash Padukone. Padukone was one of the first Indian players to make a significant impact on the international badminton scene, and he won several major titles during his career, including the All England Open in 1980. He was also the first Indian to be ranked world number one in the sport.

Another influential figure in Indian badminton is Saina Nehwal. Nehwal is a former world number one and has won several major titles, including the Commonwealth Games gold medal and the World Championship bronze medal. She is considered one of India's greatest badminton players and has inspired a generation of young players to take up the sport.

Football:

Football is another sport that has grown in popularity in India in recent years, and the country now has a thriving football league. The sport has produced several talented players over the years, and many of these players have become influential figures in Indian football.

One of the biggest influencers in Indian football is Baichung Bhutia. Bhutia is widely regarded as one of India's greatest footballers and is known for his skill and dedication to the sport. He has won numerous awards and accolades during his career, including the Arjuna Award and the Padma Shri.

Another influential figure in Indian football is Sunil Chhetri. Chhetri is the current captain of the Indian national team and is widely regarded as one of the best footballers in the country. He has scored the most goals for India in international competitions and has inspired a generation of young players to take up the sport.

Wrestling:

Wrestling has a long history in India and is considered one of the country's traditional sports. The sport has produced many talented athletes over the years, and several Indian wrestlers have become influential figures in the sport both nationally and internationally.

One of the biggest influencers in Indian wrestling is Sushil Kumar. Kumar is a two-time Olympic medalist and has won numerous international titles, including the World Wrestling Championships and the Commonwealth Games. He is widely regarded as one of India's greatest wrestling champions and has inspired a generation of young wrestlers to pursue the sport.

Another influential figure in Indian wrestling is Yogeshwar Dutt. Dutt is a former Olympic medalist and has won several international titles, including the Asian Games and the Commonwealth Games. He is known for his determination and dedication to the sport, and has inspired many young athletes to pursue wrestling.

India has a rich sporting heritage and has produced many talented athletes and sports influencers over the years. From cricket to football and from wrestling to badminton, these influencers have made a significant impact in their respective sports and inspired a generation of young athletes to pursue their passions. It is important to recognize and celebrate their contributions to Indian sports and to continue to support the growth and development of sports in the country.

౭౦

"From the fields of ancient battles to the modern-day stadiums, the legacy of Indian sports is a rich tapestry of courage and skill."

৪

VII

Traditional Indian Martial Arts

India has a rich cultural heritage and a long history of traditional martial arts. From ancient times, martial arts have been an important part of Indian life, serving both as a means of physical fitness and as a form of self-defense. These traditional martial arts are deeply rooted in Indian culture and have played a significant role in shaping the country's rich sporting heritage.

Kalarippayattu:

Kalarippayattu is one of the oldest and most respected traditional martial arts in India. It is believed to have originated in the southern state of Kerala over 2,000 years ago and is considered the mother of all Indian martial arts. Kalarippayattu is a highly sophisticated and physically demanding martial art that involves a combination of physical exercises, weapon training, and combat techniques.

The training in Kalarippayattu involves rigorous physical exercise, including running, jumping, and acrobatics. It also involves the use of weapons such as swords, spears, and shields, and the techniques are designed to be used in both individual and group combat situations. The art of Kalarippayattu is steeped in tradition and is considered a living legacy of the ancient Indian warrior culture.

Gatka:

Gatka is a traditional martial art that originated in the northern state of Punjab. It is a weapon-based art that involves the use of swords, shields, and other weapons, and is known for its fast-paced and highly athletic techniques. Gatka is widely practiced in Punjab and is an important part of Punjabi culture and tradition.

The training in Gatka involves physical exercise, weapon training, and combat techniques, and is designed to develop speed, strength, and agility. The techniques of Gatka are highly sophisticated and are designed to be used in both individual and group combat situations. Gatka is an important part of Punjabi heritage and is widely celebrated in the state during traditional festivals and cultural events.

Silambam:

Silambam is a traditional martial art that originated in the southern state of Tamil Nadu. It is a weapon-based art that involves the use of a long stick, known as a 'silambam', and is known for its fluid and graceful techniques. Silambam is widely practiced in Tamil Nadu and is an important part of Tamil cultural and sporting heritage.

The training in Silambam involves physical exercise, weapon training, and combat techniques, and is designed to develop strength, flexibility, and balance. The techniques of Silambam are designed to be used in both individual and group combat situations, and are highly regarded for their speed and precision. Silambam is an important part of Tamil Nadu's cultural heritage and is widely celebrated in the state during traditional festivals and cultural events.

Mallakhamb:

Mallakhamb is a traditional Indian sport that originated in the western state of Maharashtra. It is a form of gymnastics that involves performing acrobatic and gymnastic feats while hanging from a vertical pole. Mallakhamb is known for its combination of strength, flexibility, and balance, and is widely considered one of the most physically demanding traditional sports in India.

The training in Mallakhamb involves rigorous physical exercise and conditioning, including running, jumping, and acrobatics. The techniques of Mallakhamb are designed to develop strength, flexibility, and balance, and are highly regarded for their speed and precision. Mallakhamb is an important part of Maharashtra's cultural and sporting heritage and is widely celebrated in the state during traditional festivals and cultural events.

"The spirit of sportsmanship and fair play are deeply ingrained in the legacy of Indian sports, inspiring generations to come."

৪৩

VIII

The Economics of Indian Sports

The sports industry in India has been growing rapidly in recent years, with a significant impact on the country's economy. From professional sports teams to individual athletes, the sports industry in India generates billions of dollars in revenue each year and provides employment opportunities for thousands of people.

Professional Sports Teams:

The Indian Premier League (IPL), the country's premier professional cricket league, is one of the largest sports leagues in the world in terms of revenue. With a total of eight teams, the IPL generates millions of dollars in revenue each year from television rights, sponsorship deals, and ticket sales. The league also provides employment opportunities for hundreds of professional cricketers, as well as support staff, coaches, and administrators.

In addition to the IPL, there are several other professional sports leagues in India, including the Indian Super League (ISL) for football, the Pro Kabaddi League (PKL) for Kabaddi, and the Hockey India League (HIL) for field hockey. These leagues generate significant revenue and provide employment opportunities for athletes and support staff.

Individual Athletes:

In addition to professional sports teams, there are many individual athletes in India who have made a significant impact on the country's economy. These athletes generate revenue through endorsement deals, sponsorship agreements, and prize money from sporting events.

For example, Virat Kohli, the current captain of the Indian cricket team, is one of the highest-paid athletes in India, with an estimated net worth of over $100 million. Kohli generates millions of dollars each year from endorsement deals with companies such as Pepsi, Puma, and Audi.

Infrastructure Development:

The growth of the sports industry in India has also had a significant impact on infrastructure development in the country. The construction of sports stadiums, training facilities, and other infrastructure has provided employment opportunities and has helped to boost the local economy in many regions.

In addition, the development of sports infrastructure has helped to promote sports tourism in India. With the country's rich sporting heritage and growing reputation as a sports destination, many tourists now visit India to attend sporting events and watch their favorite athletes compete. This has helped to generate significant revenue for the country's economy and has contributed to the growth of the tourism industry.

The sports industry in India has a significant impact on the country's economy. From professional sports teams to individual athletes, the sports industry generates billions of dollars in revenue each year and provides employment opportunities for thousands of people. The growth of the sports industry has also had a significant impact on infrastructure development in the country and has helped to promote sports tourism, further contributing to the growth of the economy.

"The legacy of Indian sports is not just about winning and losing, but about the character and values that are forged in the pursuit of excellence."

ଔ

IX

The Impact of Indian Sports on Society

Sports play a significant role in the lives of people in India, and its impact extends far beyond just the playing field. The sports industry has had a profound impact on Indian society, shaping the country's cultural identity and shaping the lives of individuals in a variety of ways.

Cultural Identity:

Sports play a major role in shaping the cultural identity of India. From the ancient Olympic games in ancient Greece to the modern-day Olympic games, sports have always been a way for people to come together and celebrate their shared cultural heritage. In India, sports such as cricket and field hockey have a long and rich history, and continue to be an important part of the country's cultural heritage.

For example, cricket is widely regarded as the national sport of India, and is played and followed by millions of people across the country. Cricket is a unifying force in India, bringing people together from different regions and cultural backgrounds to support their favorite teams and players.

Social Integration:

Sports also play an important role in promoting social integration in India. Through sports, people from different regions and cultural backgrounds come together to compete and cooperate, helping to build bridges between communities and promoting greater understanding and cooperation.

For example, the national sports teams in India, such as the Indian cricket team, bring together players from different regions and cultural backgrounds to represent the country on the world stage. This helps to promote a sense of national pride and unity, and encourages people from different regions to work together towards a common goal.

Health and Wellness:

In addition to its cultural and social impact, sports also play an important role in promoting health and wellness in India. Regular physical activity and participation in sports have been shown to have a positive impact on physical and mental health, helping to reduce the risk of chronic diseases and promoting a sense of well-being.

Sports also provide a platform for individuals to develop physical and mental skills, such as teamwork, leadership, and problem-solving, which can be applied in other areas of life. This helps to build confidence and self-esteem, and can have a positive impact on an individual's overall well-being.

Economic Development:

Sports also have a significant impact on the economic development of India. The sports industry generates billions of dollars in revenue each year and provides employment opportunities for thousands of people.

In addition, the development of sports infrastructure, such as stadiums, training facilities, and other facilities, has helped to boost the local economy in many regions. The growth of the sports industry has also helped to promote sports tourism in India, further contributing to the country's economic growth.

Sports play a significant role in the lives of people in India, and its impact extends far beyond just the playing field. From shaping the country's cultural identity to promoting social integration, health, and wellness, and economic development, sports have a profound impact on Indian society. Through sports, people from different regions and cultural backgrounds come together to celebrate their shared heritage and work towards a common goal, making sports an important part of the fabric of Indian society.

"The tradition of sports in India is a testament to the nation's rich cultural heritage and the resilience of its people."

৪৩

X

The Future of Indian Sports

The future of Indian sports is bright, with the country poised to take a leading role in the global sports landscape in the coming years. With a rapidly growing population and a rich cultural heritage, India has the potential to become a major player in the sports industry, and the development of the sports sector is likely to have a significant impact on the country's economic and social development.

Infrastructure Development:

One of the key drivers of the future growth of Indian sports is the development of sports infrastructure. The Indian government has already taken steps to invest in sports infrastructure, with the construction of new stadiums, training facilities, and other facilities across the country.

These investments in sports infrastructure will help to

promote the growth of the sports industry in India and provide a platform for the country's athletes to compete on the world stage. The development of sports infrastructure will also help to boost the local economy in many regions, creating jobs and stimulating economic growth.

Sports Industry Growth:

In addition to infrastructure development, the growth of the sports industry is also likely to play a major role in the future of Indian sports. The sports industry generates billions of dollars in revenue each year and is one of the fastest-growing industries in the world.

In India, the growth of the sports industry is being driven by a number of factors, including the increasing popularity of sports such as cricket, field hockey, and kabaddi, as well as the growing number of corporate sponsorships and media rights deals. As the sports industry continues to grow, it will provide more opportunities for Indian athletes to compete at the highest level and for fans to enjoy their favorite sports.

Promoting Health and Wellness:

Another important aspect of the future of Indian sports is the role it will play in promoting health and wellness. Regular physical activity and participation in sports have been shown to have a positive impact on physical and mental health, helping to reduce the risk of chronic diseases and promoting a sense of well-being.

In the future, the growth of the sports industry in India

is likely to result in more opportunities for people to participate in sports, helping to promote health and wellness on a wider scale. The development of sports programs in schools and the promotion of physical activity from a young age will also play an important role in promoting health and wellness in the future.

Growing International Influence:

Finally, the future of Indian sports is likely to be shaped by the country's growing international influence. With India set to play host to a number of major international sports events in the coming years, including the 2023 World Cup and the 2022 Commonwealth Games, the country is poised to take a leading role in the global sports landscape.

This growing international influence is likely to result in more opportunities for Indian athletes to compete on the world stage, as well as increased investment in the sports industry and the development of sports infrastructure. It will also help to promote India as a major player in the global sports landscape, and help to shape the future of sports in the country.

The future of Indian sports is bright, with the country poised to take a leading role in the global sports landscape in the coming years. With investments in sports infrastructure, the growth of the sports industry, the promotion of health and wellness, and the country's growing international influence, the future of Indian sports looks bright and full of promise.

ॐ

"The legacy of Indian sports is a proud symbol of the country's determination to succeed, both on and off the field."

XI

The Legacy of Indian Sports

The Indian subcontinent has a rich and vibrant sports culture that has evolved over the centuries. From ancient times, the people of India have been passionate about physical activity and have developed a variety of traditional sports that are an integral part of the country's heritage. From wrestling and martial arts to archery and horse riding, these traditional sports have played an important role in shaping the cultural identity of India and are an important part of the legacy of Indian sports.

One of the most famous traditional sports in India is wrestling. Wrestling has been a popular sport in India for thousands of years and has been mentioned in Hindu scripture, including the Mahabharata and the Ramayana. The sport was typically held during religious and cultural festivals, and was seen as a means of demonstrating strength and courage. Wrestling was also used as a way of preparing soldiers for battle and was considered an important aspect of warrior training.

Martial arts is another traditional sport that has a rich history in India. The Indian martial arts style known as Kalarippayattu originated in the southern part of the country and is one of the oldest forms of martial arts in the world. The sport involves a combination of physical skills, such as hand-to-hand combat and weapons training, and spiritual and mental training, including meditation and yoga. Kalarippayattu is still widely practiced in India today and is considered an important part of the country's cultural heritage.

Archery is another ancient sport that has been a part of Indian culture for thousands of years. Archery was traditionally used as a means of hunting and warfare, but it also became a popular form of sport and recreation. In India, archery was often associated with royalty and was seen as a symbol of power and prestige. Today, archery remains a popular sport in India and is an important part of the country's athletic legacy.

Horse riding is another traditional sport that has a long history in India. The sport was initially developed by Indian royalty as a means of demonstrating their wealth and power. Over time, horse riding became an important part of Indian culture and was often associated with nobility and prestige. Today, horse riding remains a popular sport in India and is enjoyed by people of all ages and backgrounds.

In addition to these traditional sports, India has also produced a number of world-class athletes in a variety of modern sports. From field hockey and cricket to badminton and gymnastics, Indian athletes have made their mark on the international stage and have helped to establish India as a major player in the world of sports.

The legacy of Indian sports is rich and diverse, encompassing a wide range of traditional and modern sports. From wrestling and martial arts to archery and horse riding, these sports have played an important role in shaping the cultural identity of India and are an important part of the country's athletic heritage. As the world becomes increasingly connected, the legacy of Indian sports continues to inspire and captivate people around the globe.

More Quotes on Indian Traditional Sports

"Sports have the power to bring people together, and the legacy of Indian sports is a shining example of unity in diversity."

"The legacy of Indian sports is not just about the achievements of great athletes, but about the spirit of teamwork and camaraderie."

"The story of Indian sports is one of overcoming obstacles and breaking barriers, inspiring us all to strive for greatness."

"The legacy of Indian sports is a testament to the country's rich history, diverse culture, and enduring spirit."

"The pursuit of excellence in sports has been a cornerstone of the Indian identity, and the legacy of Indian sports will continue to inspire future generations."

"The legacy of Indian sports is a celebration of the human spirit, and a testament to the power of hard work and determination."

"Sports have the power to bring people together, and the legacy of Indian sports is a

shining example of unity in diversity."

"The legacy of Indian sports is a symbol of the country's cultural richness, diversity, and enduring spirit."

"The history of Indian sports is one of triumph, perseverance, and resilience, inspiring us all to strive for greatness in all aspects of our lives."

৪৩

OTHER BOOKS OF THE AUTHOR

1. The Moments When I Met God
2. Kashiyile Theertha Pathangal
3. GURU GYAN VANI
4. Abhiprerak Gita
5. ASSI SE JAIN GHAT TAK
6. Hopelessness of Arjuna
7. The Soul and It's True Nature
8. Sense of Action (Karma)
9. Action through Wisdom
10. Action through Wisdom
11. THEORY AND PRACTICAL OF EVERY ACTION
12. LOGICAL UNDERSTANDING OF THE SUPREME
13. THE IMPERISHABLE SUPREME
14. Yatra Nishadraj se Hanuman Ghat Tak
15. Yatra Karnatak Ghat se Raja Ghat Tak
16. Yatra Pandey Ghat se Prayagraj Ghat Tak
17. Yatra Ranjendra Prasad Ghat se Dattatreya Ghat Tak
18. YaatraSindhiya Ghat se Gwaliar Ghat Tak
19. Yatra Mangala Gauri Ghat se Hanuman Gadhi Ghat Tak
20. Yatra Gaay Ghat Se Nishad Ghat Tak
21. MAA GANGA, GHATEN EVM UTSAV
22. Ganga Arti Dev Deepavali evam Any Utsav
23. Potentials of Digitalized India
24. VEDIC CONSCIOUSNESS
25. A Brief Introduction to Vedic Science
26. Kashi ke Barah Jyotirling
27. IMPACT OF MOTIVATION
28. Let's have a Milky Way Journey
29. Color Therapy in a Nutshell

30. Rigveda in a Nutshell
31. Yajurveda in a Nutshell
32. Samveda in a Nutshell
33. Atharva Veda in a Nutshell
34. Ayushman Bhava - Ayurveda
35. Srimad Bhagavad Gita and Upanishad Connection
36. Srimad Bhagavad Gita - an attempt to summarize each chapter.
37. Facts and Impact of Nakshatra
38. Astro Gems - NAVARATNA
39. Ekadashi - A Concise Overview
40. A Concise View of Hanuman Chalisa
41. Inspirational Gita
42. Nakshatraranyam
43. Summary of 18 Mahapuranas
44. Synopsis of 18 Upa Puranas
45. Rigvediya Upanishads
46. Shukla Yajurvediya Upanishads
47. Krishna Yajurvediya Upanishads
48. Samavediya Upanishads
49. Atharvavediya Upanishads
50. The Seven Great Sages
51. From Rocket Scientist to President Dr. APJ Abdul Kalam
52. The Visionary's Voice - Quotes of Dr. APJ Abdul Kalam
53. The Wisdom of Swami Vivekananda: Insights and Inspiration from a Legendary Spiritual Teacher
54. Ayurvedic Remedies from the Garden
55. Sages and Seers
56. Rising Strong – Motivational Stories of Women
57. Beyond Flames -Mystery stories of Funeral Ghat Manikarnika
58. The Origins of Tulsi: A Look at the Mythological Roots of the Plant"

163. The Indian Royal Kitchens: A Gastronomic Journey Through the Kitchens of India's Maharajas
164. The Indian Sports: An Insight into the History and Significance of Indian Traditional Sports

CONTACT

DR. JAGADEESH PILLAI

MBA & PhD in Vedic Science

Four Times Guinness World Record Holder

Winner of Mahatma Gandhi Vishwa Shanti Puraskar and
Global Peace Ambassador

Gemology, Astro & Vastu Consultant - Spiritual Counselor

Consultant for designing World Record Ideas

Efficient Tarot Card Reader

9839093003

myrichindia@gmail.com

drjagadeeshpillai@facebook

drjagadeeshpillai@instagram
jagadeeshpillai@youtube

www. JAGADEESHPILLAI.com